Lake District: **Ridge** Walks &
Scrambles

Text: *Carl Rogers*
Photographs: *Carl Rogers, Shutterstock, Dreamstime*

Design: *Carl Rogers*

© Northern Eye Books Limited 2021

Carl Rogers has asserted his rights under the Copyright, Designs and Patents Act, 1988 to be identified as the authors of this work. All rights reserved.

This book contains mapping data licensed from the Ordnance Survey with the permission of the Controller of Her Majesty's Stationery Office. © Crown copyright 2021 All rights reserved. Licence number 100047867

Northern Eye Books
ISBN 978-1-908632-83-8

A CIP catalogue record for this book is available from the British Library.

Cover: *Scramblers on Striding Edge, Helvellyn (route 9). Shutterstock*

The routes described in this book are undertaken at the reader's own risk. Walkers should take into account their level of fitness, wear suitable footwear and clothing, and carry food and water. It is also advisable to take the relevant OS map with you in case you get lost and leave the area covered by our maps.

Whilst every care has been taken to ensure the accuracy of the route directions, the publishers cannot accept responsibility for errors or omissions, or for changes in the details given. Nor can the publisher and copyright owners accept responsibility for any consequences arising from the use of this book.

If you find any inaccuracies in either the text or maps, please write or email us at the address below. Thank you.

First published in 2016. 2nd Edition 2021

Northern Eye Books Limited
Northern Eye Books, Tattenhall, Cheshire CH3 9PX
Email: tony@northerneyebooks.com

For sales enquiries, please call 01928 723 744

@northerneyebooks
@carlrogers1960

@CarlMarabooks
@Northerneyeboo

Contents

Cockermouth
Bassenthwaite Lake
Skiddaw
Blencathra
10
Penrith
A66
A66
Lorton
Keswick
Braithwaite
Grisedale Pike
5
Derwent Water
Loweswater
Grasmoor
Crummock Water
Buttermere
6
Borrowdale
Glenridding
Ullswater
4
Thirlmere
Helvellyn
9
Patterdale
Ennerdale Water
Buttermere
Haweswater
Ennerdale
3
Pillar
8
Great Gable
Fairfield
High Street
7
L A K E   D I S T R I C T
1
A591
Wasdale
Scafell Pike
Bowfell
Langdale
Grasmere
2
Wast Water
Ambleside
Eskdale
Troutbeck
Old Man of Coniston
Hawkshead
Windermere
Windermere
Coniston

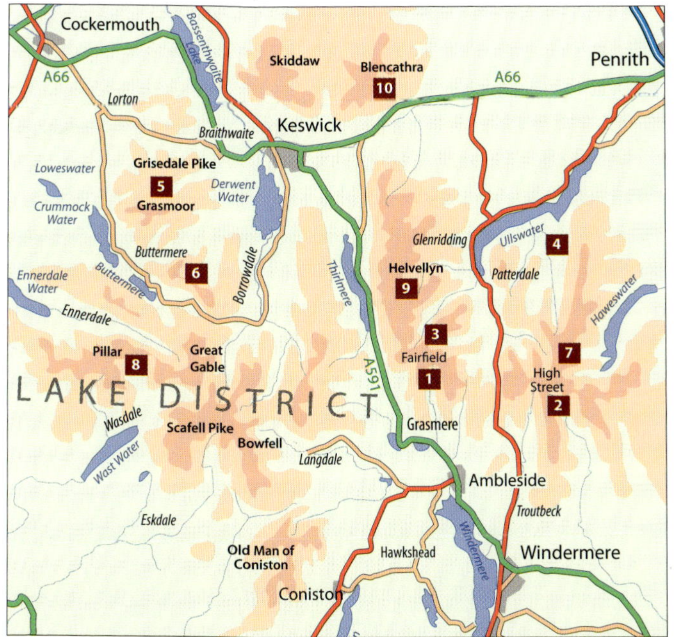

England's largest National Park

The **Lake District National Park** is the largest and most popular of the thirteen National Parks in England and Wales. Created as one of Britain's first National Parks in 1951, its role is to 'conserve and enhance' the natural beauty, wildlife and culture of this iconic English landscape, not just for residents and visitors today but for future generations, too.

Remarkably, the National Park contains every scrap of England's land over 3,000 feet, including its highest mountain, Scafell Pike. Packed within the Park's 885 square miles are numerous peaks and fells, over 400 lakes and tarns, around 50 dales, six National Nature Reserves, and more than 100 Sites of Special Scientific Interest — all publicly accessible on over 1,800 miles of footpaths and other rights of way. It's no surprise then, that the Lake District attracts an estimated 15 million visitors a year.

Striding Edge, Helvellyn

Lakeland ridges

The Lakeland Fells have some of the finest ridge walks in the country. Exploring these ridges offers fell walking at its most satisfying — staying high, taking in several summits and enjoying the spectacular settings.

Many of the Lake District's ridge walks have become classics, like the grassy edges of the Fairfield and Kentmere Horseshoes, or the rocky aretes of Striding Edge and Swirral Edge, and the aptly named Sharp Edge of Blencathra.

"[The fells], towering above each other, or lifting themselves in ridges like the waves of a tumultuous sea ... are surpassed by none."

William Wordsworth

TOP 10 **Walks:** Ridge Walks and Scrambles

The ten routes outlined in the following pages are amongst the very best ridge walks and scrambles to be enjoyed on the Lakeland Fells. Some are well known classics like the Fairfield or Kentmere Horseshoes, while others are surprisingly well kept secrets like the wonderful Mosedale Horseshoe, the Boredale Horseshoe, the Rough Crag ridge, or the circuit of Deepdale. Also included are Lakeland's most challenging ridge scrambles: Helvellyn's Striding Edge and Swirral Edge, and the dramatic Sharp Edge on Blencathra.

Coledale Horseshoe
page 32
Little Dale Round
page 38
High Street by Rough Crag
page 42
Mosedale Horseshoe
page 46
SCRAMBLE
Striding & Swirral Edges
page 52
SCRAMBLE
Blencathra's ridges
page 58

Fairfield's grassy ridge stretches away into the cloud

Fairfield Horseshoe

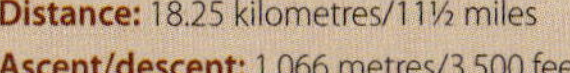
*Low Sweden Bridge – Low Pike – High Pike – Dove Crag –
Hart Crag – Fairfield – Great Rigg – Heron Pike – Nab Scar*

What to expect:
*Good paths on a broad,
high ridge. Steep descent*

Distance: 18.25 kilometres/11½ miles

Ascent/descent: 1,066 metres/3,500 feet

Start: Pay and Display car park at the northern end of Ambleside,
on the A591.

Grid ref: NY 376 046

Ordnance Survey Map: OL 5 The English Lakes North-eastern area,
and OL 7 The English Lakes South-eastern area

Wainwrights: Low Pike, High Pike, Dove Crag, Hart Crag, Fairfield,
Great Rigg, Heron Pike, Nab Scar

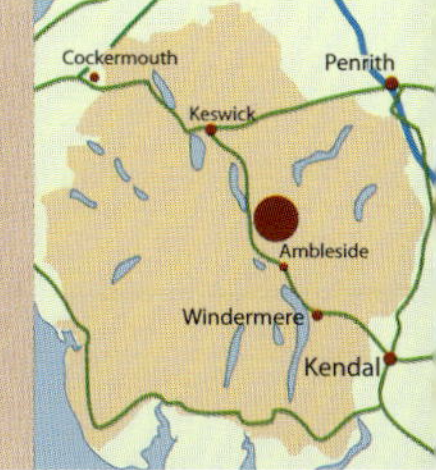

Walk outline

*Low Sweden Bridge provides the key for gaining the ridge
that rises above Scandale. Once reached, this entertaining
ridge takes you over progressively higher summits from Low
Pike over High Pike, Dove Crag, Hart Crag and eventually the
lofty plateau of Fairfield. From here the western arm of the
horseshoe is followed in a southerly direction over Great Rigg,
Heron Pike, and finally the end of the ridge at Nab Scar. From
here, a steep descent leads to Rydal, where a track passes
through Rydal Park, taking you back to Ambleside.*

Looking ahead

Fairfield Horseshoe

The Fairfield Horseshoe is one of the best known ridge
walks in the Lake District and as such is on every fell walker's
'must do' list. Its fame and popularity is well deserved, eight
summits linked by a graceful undulating ridge with not too
much height loss between and wide views in every direction.
Satisfaction guaranteed.

In spring, watch for wheatears returning from overwintering in
Africa to feed on the short turf of these high ridges.

Wheatear

A fell runner heading along the high, rock-strewn ridge

The Walk

1. Leave the car park over the **footbridge** and cross the road. Turn left, then immediately right uphill on the 'Kirkstone Pass' road. Take the first left turning and keep to the left when the lane forks. Walk down **Nook Lane**, signposted for 'Low Sweden Bridge'.

Continue to **Nook End Farm**, go through gates to the right of the farmhouse, and cross the farmyard. Continue along the track to cross **Low Sweden Bridge**.

2. Continue on the broad rising track, eventually passing through a gate in the wall. Curve to the left, with the wall on your the left, and continue through two wall gaps.

Bear left at a fork just after the second gap, and continue along the ridge with the wall on your left.

Continue to a **cairn at the base of crags**, and scramble up a tricky step beside the wall. (The step can be avoided by cutting right, up the rocks, just before it). Carry on beside the wall, go through a gap, and continue over broken ground. Leave the wall for a while to avoid boggy ground. Return to the wall, go through a low gap, and climb to a cairn.

Bear left, a little further on, leaving the good path and taking a fainter one that stays with the wall and climbs to **Low Pike summit**.

3. From the cairn, head east, dropping down to curve left below the summit. Descend to a saddle, and cross a stile over a wall. When the wall on the left ends against crags, step over it, and continue on the other side; the wall reappears on your right. Stay beside the wall, eventually passing through a gap, to reach the **summit cairn on High Pike**.

Return to the wall, staying on the right of it now, dropping briefly before climbing steeply. As the angle eases, the wall becomes broken; continue on the path to the rocky **summit of Dove Crag**.

4. Descend on the right of the broken wall to a saddle. Climb steep rough ground, with the wall still on the left, to the twin cairns on the **summit of Hart Crag**.

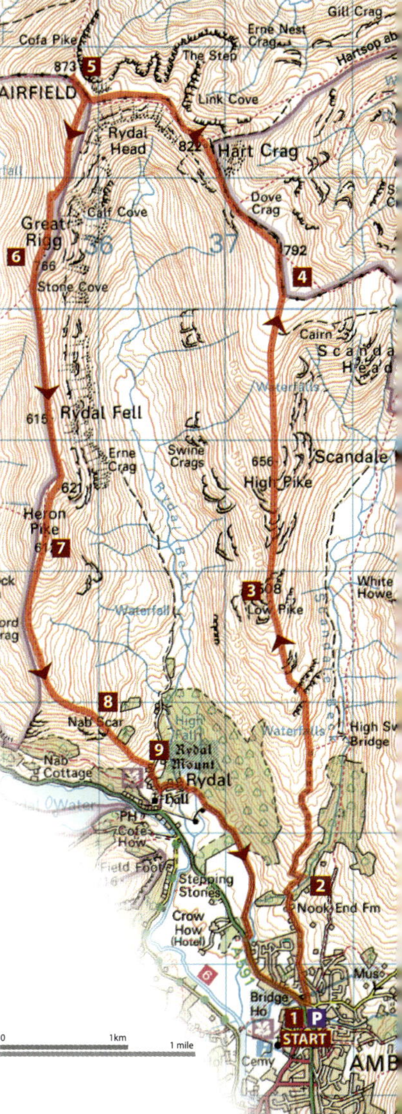

A walker watches as Fairfield and Great Rigg emerge from the cloud

Descend on a good path to a high-level saddle. Continue in the same direction, climbing steeply over a **rocky knoll**, to curve left and walk across the **Fairfield** summit plateau. Curve right along the path to reach the **summit**, where there is a **stone wind shelter**.

5. From the summit, head south across the plateau (in the direction of distant Windermere) to pick up the ridge path. Follow this path along the broad ridge to the **summit of Great Rigg** — a straightforward 1 kilometre/¾ mile.

6. Continue south along the ridge from Great Rigg — easy walking all the way — to a broad saddle before the short climb to Heron Pike. Climb steadily from the saddle leaving the main path beyond a **little tarn** on the left, to take a fainter path, half-left, to **Heron Pike's north top**. Continue on the fainter path, to rejoin the main path. Drop down, then climb again, to reach **Heron Pike south summit**.

7. From Heron Pike the ridge path continues in the same direction — still easy and straightforward — to pick up a broken wall on the right. Continue to **Nab Scar,** and then meander along the summit ridge to a **cairn** where the old wall ends.

8. Continue ahead, crossing a stile in the wall, to follow the path beyond, now with a wall on the right. Drop steeply down the zig-zag path, which lower down joins a walled track. Continue along the track towards buildings below. Descend to pass through a gate and walk down a drive to a lane.

9. Turn right along the lane to the entrance to **Rydal Hall**. Turn left, on a footpath signposted to 'Ambleside'. Follow the track to the left of the buildings, and then right and left, past a **teashop**.

Cut left through the **campsite**, following the signs, and continue through a gate beside a stile. Follow the track ahead through **Rydal Park** to the main **A591** beside the **old lodge**.

Cross the road, and turn left along the pavement back into **Ambleside**, to complete the route. ♦

On the first half of the Kentmere Horseshoe

Kentmere Horseshoe

Garburn Pass – Yoke – Ill Bell – Froswick – Thornthwaite Crag – High Street – Nan Bield Pass – Kentmere Pike

Distance: 21 kilometres/13 miles

Ascent/descent: 1,210 metres/3,910 feet

Start: Limited parking in Kentmere village. A handful of cars can be parked by the institute by the church. Begin the walk by the church

Grid ref: NY 457 041

Ordnance Survey Map: OL 7 The English Lakes South-eastern area. *Windermere, Kendal & Silverdale*

Wainwrights: Yoke, Ill Bell, Froswick, Thornthwaite Crag, High Street, Mardale Ill Bell, Harter Fell, Kentmere Pike, Shipman Knotts

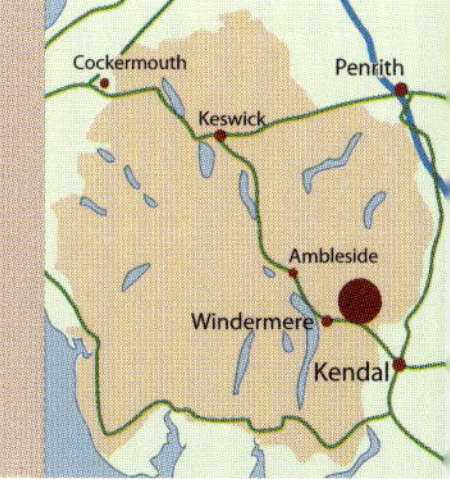

Walk outline

Easy walking from Kentmere village on a bridleway leads onto the broad ridge. A steeper rise to the first summit is followed by superb ridge walking on good paths with extensive views. The second half of the horseshoe is less interesting and can be left out if needed, but this would change the character of the walk. The final few miles are easy with the gradual descent of a broad gentle ridge with farm tracks back to Kentmere.

Kentmere Horseshoe

This route is a ridge walker's dream. Once the main ridge is gained most of the work is done and you can enjoy miles of elevated walking on good paths with minimal effort between summits and stunning views west towards Helvellyn and St Sunday Crag, and southwest to the long finger of Windermere. Although quite a long circuit, there is minimal rise and fall between each summit and with good paths under foot the miles slip by surprisingly easily. The second half of the horseshoe can be left out with an easier return along the valley from the Nan Bield Pass if needed.

In summer, the skyward trill of skylarks sometimes fills the air on Lakeland's high fells, lifting the spirits.

Summit of High Street

Skylark

Looking back to Froswick and Ill Bell from the approach to High Street

The Walk

1. From the **church** follow the lane away from the village and take the first lane on the left. In about 150 metres, and immediately after the house '**Green Head**' on the right, turn right onto the path signed for '**Garburn Pass**'. The path rises as a wide **cobbled track** (an old lane over the fells to Troutbeck), passing a huge boulder in the field on the left known as '**Badger Rock**', a well known local landmark.

Follow the track up onto the rounded crest of the ridge where you pass through a gate almost at the highest point. In 100 metres or so, turn right on a grass path that heads directly across the boggy, sloping moors roughly parallel to the **wall** away to the right. Further on, the path runs close by the wall and you meet a broad surfaced path that continues the climb to the first summit of the day — **Yoke**.

This summit is a broad grassy plateau marked by a single cairn, but it gives you your first proper views of the ridge ahead, and the fine shapely summit of Ill Bell.

2. The well-made path continues along

the narrowing ridge crest to the **summit of Ill Bell** with its collection of stone cairns and view down to the **Kentmere Reservoir**.

Almost the entire walk can now be seen — the continuation to Froswick and Thornthwaite Crag, and High Street at the head of the Kentmere valley, and the second half of the ridge beyond the Nan Bield Pass over Harter Fell and Kentmere Pike.

The path continues over the less interesting summit of **Froswick** then along the connecting ridge to **Thornthwaite Crag** where the line of the old **Roman road** reaches the ridge from Troutbeck.

Thornthwaite Crag is an expansive summit with a tall stone cairn. Like Ill Bell it would be hard to mistake this top even in the poorest visibility. In clear weather its central location gives it grand views west to Helvellyn, St Sunday Crag and Dove Crag, and north down to Ullswater. South, the view includes Ill Bell and Froswick rising above the Kentmere valley.

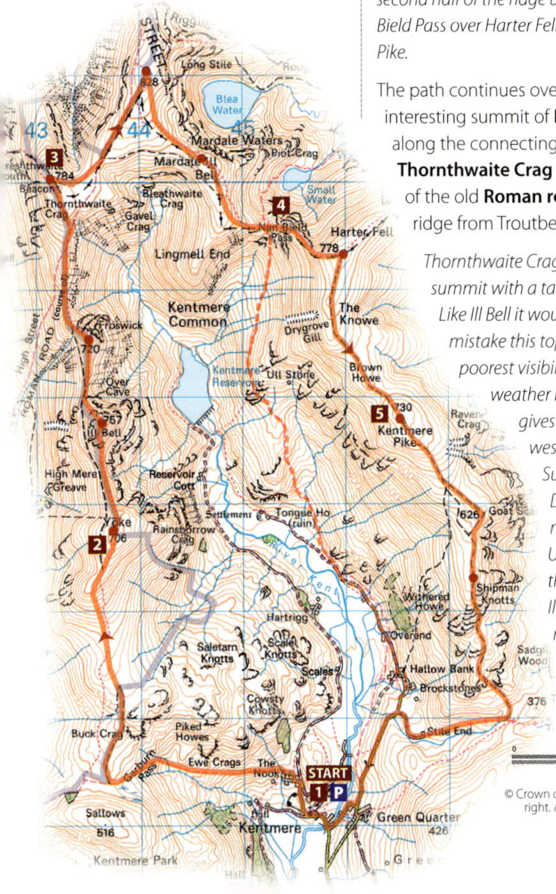

Once the climbing is done you can enjoy miles of elevated walking

3. From Thornthwaite Crag the path curves east, then north with views down to **Hayeswater**. The main path is approximately on the line of the Roman road here and is probably wide enough to accommodate a marching army. As you approach **High Street**, break away right to reach the summit marked by an **Ordnance Survey triangulation pillar**.

Views from the summit are restricted by the wide flat expanse of grass, but a short walk east to the lip of Blea Water Crag gives a grand view down into the head of Mardale with both Blea Water and Haweswater visible below.

Bear right now along the edge of the broken cliffs that fall to **Blea Water** to the next summit — **Mardale III Bell** — an indistinct rise on the broad moors but with excellent views left to the northern slopes of High Street rising above Blea Water — the deepest tarn in the Lake District at 63 metres/207 feet. A little further on the path drops to **Nan Bield Pass**, an ancient route over the fells marked by a s**quare stone wind shelter**.

(The walk could be cut short here if necessary by following the zig-zag path to the right. This heads across the

slopes of Harter Fell above the Kentmere Reservoir, then along the valley bottom to join the lane end near the farms of Hallow Bank and Brockstones. Follow the lane back to Kentmere.)

4. The climb out of the Nan Bield Pass to the broad summit of **Harter Fell** is soon over. The highest point is marked by a **cairn** and close by is a **fence** which divides the broad ridge.

Follow the path right beside the fence for almost 2 kilometres/1¼ miles, the slight fall and rise to **Kentmere Pike** barely noticed.

5. From Kentmere Pike the path continues beside the wall southeast for just over 1 kilometre/¾ mile to cross a ladder stile in a crossing wall. **Shipman Knotts**, little more than a slight rise on the ridge, marks the final summit of the day. From here the path continues south beside the wall to join the **old track** linking Kentmere with Longsleddale. Turn right and follow the track down to the tarmac lane in the **Kentmere** valley. Turn left along the lane for about 1 kilometre/¾ mile and take the first lane on the right. Follow this down to the T-junction and turn right to return to the church to complete the route. ♦

Sunrise over Fairfield seen from St Sunday Crag

Deepdale Horseshoe

*Patterdale – Birks – St Sunday Crag – Deepdale Hause –
Cofa Pike – Fairfield – Hart Crag – Hartsop Above How*

What to expect:
*Steep ascent on good
paths. High-level stony
and grassy paths*

Distance: 14.5 kilometres/9 miles

Ascent/descent: 1050 metres/3,400 feet

Start: Small pay and display car park opposite the 'Patterdale Hotel',
Patterdale

Grid ref: NY 396 159

Ordnance Survey Map: OL 5 The English Lakes North-eastern area.
Penrith, Patterdale & Caldbeck

Wainwrights: St Sunday Crag, Fairfield, Hart Crag, Hartsop Above
How (Birks optional)

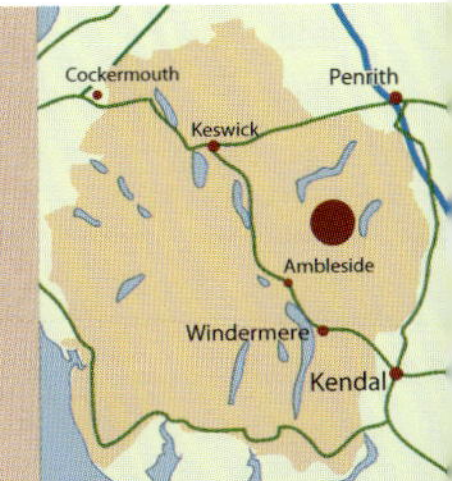

Walk outline

*After a gentle start in Patterdale, a steep climb up Thornhow
End takes you onto the broad stocky summit ridge of St
Sunday Crag with its superb views of Helvellyn and its
impressive eastern ridges. With much of the height gained the
walking is easier along the ridge with a short simple scramble
over Cofa Pike to reach Fairfield's broad summit plateau. The
broad ridge is followed to Hart Crag, then abandoned in
favour of the long gentle arm of Hartsop Above How with its
excellent views into the wilds of upper Deepdale.*

Cofa Pike

Deepdale Horseshoe

Fairfield sits at the centre of a complex of fells, ridges and
dales running to all points of the compass. With several
close neighbours — some major summit themselves —
the Fairfield group is perfect for ridge walking and boasts
two of the best 'horseshoe' rounds in the region: the
Fairfield Horseshoe, which takes in the southern ridges
centred on Rydal, and the Deepdale Horseshoe to the
northeast.

This is the realm of ravens whose deep, guttural calls often
echo from the cliffs and rocks.

Raven

Tackling the initial climb onto the shoulder of Birks

The Walk

1. From the car park cross the road and walk through the **hotel car park** keeping to the right of the main building. Take the signed footpath behind the hotel which passes through a small **wood** to a kissing gate. Go through the gate and bear right to follow a contouring path for about 1 kilometre/¾ mile.

At a path junction immediately below the steep, blunt ridge of **Thornhow End** (grid ref: NY 387 157), turn left. The path is steep and gains height quickly with widening views as you climb, both behind to the curve of Ullswater and right into the deepening shadowy depths of Grisedale and across to the bulk of Birkhouse Moor and Striding Edge.

2. Higher up the angle eases and the path heads for the shoulder of **Birks**, reaching the ridge midway between Birks and St Sunday Crag. (Birks can be reached easily by an out-and-back walk along the ridge to the left.)

Continue to climb directly up the broad ridge to the summit of **St Sunday Crag**.

St Sunday Crag is superb for views down into Grisedale and across to the edges of Helvellyn, Nethermost Pike and Dollywaggon Pike, as well as across Deepdale to the northern cliffs of Fairfield and Hart Crag.

3. The path crosses the broad summit dome in a southwest direction making the short descent to **Deepdale Hause**, where the paths from Grisedale and Deepdale meet. The continuation to Fairfield is up a broken rocky ridge; a steadying hand

needed here and there as you scramble up and over the rocky summit of **Cofa Pike**. It is a short climb now to the broad, bulky **summit of Fairfield**.

Leaving the summit of St Sunday Crag and heading towards Farifield

4. Fairfield sits at the junction of several ridges and provides the highpoint of both this round and the more famous Fairfield Horseshoe. *Its broad summit plateau dominates the valley heads of both Rydal Beck and Deepdale and gives grand views of virtually every fell in the Lake District.* The summit itself is close to the northern crags and is marked by a modest **stone wind shelter**.

To continue, head southeast for a few hundred metres, then pick up the broad path that swings east, then southeast along the broad ridge, soon with views right into Rydal. There is a short descent into the gap of **Link Hause** before the rise to **Hart Crag**, the third major summit of the day.

Like Fairfield, Hart Crag is a broad, stony summit and it is not always easy to decide on the highest point (just to the right of the main path).

5. The main ridge path continues southeast to **Dove Crag**, but our way heads northeast aiming for the long finger-like edge of **Hartsop Above How**. In clear conditions you will be able to see the lower section of the ridge below and you should have no problem locating it, but things will be more tricky in poor visibility.

Head northeast (on a bearing of approx. 60 degrees) from the summit to locate the cairned path that descends through steep rocky ground. Once over this, the long central section of the ridge is straightforward and enjoyable.

6. Lower down a **wall** follows the ridge crest. Stay within sight of this on the right until you are almost at the bottom of the ridge approaching woods ahead. The path trends left away from the wall here to reach a small **gate** in the fence. Go through the gate and walk down through **woods** to go through a second gate into a large field. Go ahead across the field to a farm track and follow this rightwards to the road at **Deepdale Bridge**.

Turn left along the road and return past the **Youth Hostel** to **Patterdale** to complete the route. ♦

Boredale and Place Fell

Boredale Horseshoe

St Peters Church – Howe Grain – Howstead Brow – Beda Fell – Boredale Hause – Place Fell – Bordedale

Distance: 12.5 kilometres/7¾ miles
Ascent/descent: 776 metres/2,545 feet
Start: Small layby beside St Peters Church, on the summit of the little pass separating Howtown from Martindale. (As an alternative, Howtown can be reached by steamer from Patterdale with a descent from Place Fell back to Patterdale via Boredale Hause)
Grid ref: NY 432 182
Ordnance Survey Map: OL 5 The English Lakes North-eastern area. *Penrith, Patterdale & Caldbeck*
Wainwrights: Beda Fell & Place Fell

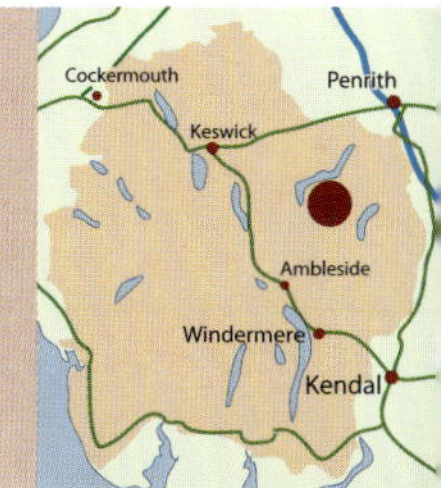

Walk outline

Beginning at St Peters Church in Martindale, the route heads down to the ancient Church of St Martin in Howe Grain, before a climb up onto the Beda Fell ridge. A narrow, grassy edge then leads, impressively, between the isolated dales of Boredale and Bannerdale to Boredale Hause overlooking Patterdale. From there a steep climb and increasingly impressive views take you up onto Place Fell with its stunning panorama of the Helvellyn range and Ullswater, before a gentle descent back to Boredale to complete the route.

Old Church of St Martin

Boredale fells

The remote far eastern fells and the deep isolated dales that cut into their heart often come as a very welcome surprise to many who consider themselves to be seasoned fell walkers. Ullswater acts like a defensive moat, protecting these fells from the hordes that gather at Cumbrian honeypots elsewhere.

Keep a look out for the red deer which can often be seen far below in Bannerdale, around The Nab. The herd is the oldest native red deer herd in England.

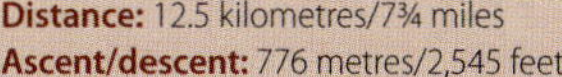

Red deer

The Walk

1. From **St Peters Church**, walk through the little car park past the church and bear right on a path beside the wall. Where the path bears left away from the wall, keep right passing a **small pool** (named as 'Lanty Tarn' on the map) and follow the wall as it swings right and through a gate in the corner. The path passes a **bench** and heads left passing a **cottage** and continuing to reach the lane. Go ahead along the lane to reach the **Old Church of St Martin**.

The earliest reference to a church here is in a charter of 1220, which also makes reference to an even earlier chapel on the same site. The present building dates from around the end of the sixteenth

Looking back to Howstead Brow from the ridge below Beda Head

century and despite its appearance has undergone several renovations. Notable features include the church bell, said to be over 500 years old, the font, which is believed to be part of a Roman altar taken from a shrine which once stood beside the nearby Roman road over High Street, and the enormous yew tree behind the church estimated to be 1,300 years old!

From the old church, continue along the lane crossing the bridge over **Howegrain Beck** and bear right up the access at **Wintercrag Farm**. Beyond the barns, take the narrow footpath ahead that climbs up beside a **wall** on the right. The path stays with the wall where it swings right to rise diagonally up the fellside to the ridge crest where there is a **metal bench**.

There are superb views into Boredale and the second half of the route over Place Fell from here.

2. Turn left along the ridge crest, making the short rise over **Howstead Brow**. The walking is easy now with fine views but soon steepens to reach the summit of **Beda Head**, the highest point on the long ridge of **Beda Fell**.

Looking along the ridge to Beda Fell and Place Fell from Howestead Brow

The continuation along the ridge crest is surprisingly good — easy-angled, narrow enough to be interesting and with fine views into both Bannerdale and Boredale.

3. In around 1 kilometer, there is a short rise towards **Beda Fell Knott** where an obvious path crosses the ridge. This is part of an old route across the fells linking Bannerdale to Patterdale. Bear right here and follow the path below the ridge crest and down to **Boredale Hause**.

Boredale Hause is a meeting of several paths, but the continuation to **Place Fell** is clear enough — a broad footpath that curves up the steep southern flanks to the sub-summit of **Round How**. From there the going is more gentle across the hummocky summit plateau to the highest point marked by a **triangulation pillar**.

Place Fell gives superb views to the Helvellyn range with Ullswater wrapped around the western slopes of the fell. At nine miles long, Ullswater is the second largest sheet of water in the Lake District with a maximum depth of just over 200 feet.

4. (If you arrived at Howtown by the steamer, return to Boredale Hause and take the Patterdale path.) Otherwise,

turn your back on the Helvellyn range and head northeast. The path passes to the left of a small, **nameless tarn** and along the crest of **Hart Crag** before descending to the boggy saddle of **Low Moss** passing an **old sheep fold** and ignoring a left fork. The path now contours the southeastern flanks of **High Dodd**.

5. In around 800 metres, as the path levels off, turn right on a path that cuts down the steep fellside, zig-zagging lower down to a stile in the wall close to a **stone barn**.

Cross the stile and turn right immediately over a second stile. Go left now, passing the barn before swinging right through the gate in the corner and down to cross a little **stone footbridge** over **Boredale Beck**. Bear left along a farm track to reach the lane beside 'Garth Head'.

The shortest route back is straight ahead, steeply up on to Howstead Brow to join the outward route at the bench on the ridge crest. Longer, but less strenuous, would be to go left along the lane, ignoring a left and continuing to cross the bridge over **Howgrain Beck**. Continue straight ahead at the fork for St Peters Church to complete the walk. ♦

Grisedale Pike

Coledale Horseshoe

Braithwaite – Grisedale Pike – Hopegill Head – Coledale Hause – Eel Crag – Sail – Scar Crags – Causey Pike

What to expect:
A mixture of grassy and rocky fell paths. Long ridge walk, several ascents/descents

Distance: 17 kilometres/10½ miles

Ascent/descent: 1,115 metres /3,660 feet

Start: There is limited free parking in an old quarry on the lefthand side of the Whinlatter Pass road (the B5292) north of Braithwaite

Grid ref: NY 227 237

Ordnance Survey Map: OL 4 The English Lakes North-western area. *Keswick, Cockermouth & Wigton*

Wainwrights: Grisedale Pike, Hopegill Head, Eel Crag, Sail, Scar Crags, Causey Pike

Walk outline

Good paths abound on the Coledale Horseshoe and the three mile ascent from Braithwaite to Grisedale Pike is no exception. With most of the hard work behind you, a good path then takes you along Hobcarton Crag to Hopegill Head with a drop to Coledale Hause. A climb of roughly five hundred feet on good paths and you are on the high point of the day: Eel Crag, at the head of Coledale. From here, a grassy ridge takes you down the southern side of the valley, crossing Sail, Scar Crags and Causey Pike, before an exciting descent and a bit of road walking brings you back to Braithwaite.

Hopegill Head

Coledale Horseshoe

The traditional circuit leaves the high level route at Sail Pass, descending to cross High Moss and returning by the Outerside to Barrow ridge. While this gives a genuine round of Coledale, it misses out three great summits that make a complete high-level horseshoe. In contrast, this extended Coledale round follows the skyline higher up to include Sail, Scar Crags and Causey Pike. On a warm day you'll be able to watch buzzards searching for thermals.

Buzzard

The Walk

1. Leave the car park up steps signposted to 'Grisedale Pike'. Curve left near a **conifer plantation**, and climb up to cross a stile in the fence. Continue ahead and stay right when the path forks. Keeping the trees on your right, climb steeply up the broad path.

When the trees end, walk ahead. The path levels along the **Kinn Ridge**, before descending into a shallow saddle. Follow the path up onto **Sleet How** to curve left along the narrowing east ridge, with a final steep and airy rise to **Grisedale Pike summit**.

2. From Grisedale Pike, descend to the southwest beside a broken wall. Drop left on a steep section, trending back to the right, to pick up the wall again. Cross a saddle, climbing up and over **Hobcarton Crag**.

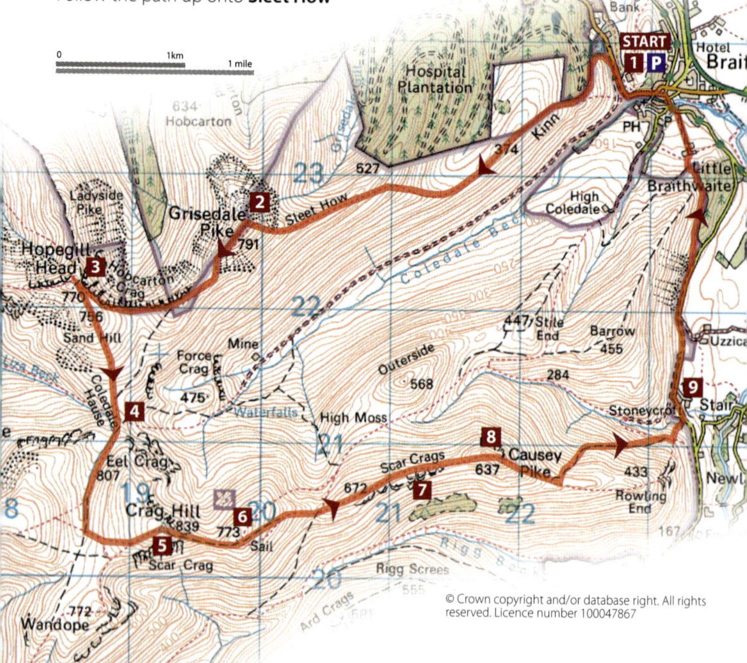

Looking along the ridge from Scar Crags to Causey Pike

Descend steeply to the saddle below **Hopegill Head,** bearing right at a **cairn** where the path forks. Climb the path above the north face of Hopegill Head, continuing to the **cairn on the rocky summit**.

3. Backtrack a little before branching off to the right, southwards, crossing **Sand Hill** on a broad path. Descend to **Coledale Hause,** at first on scree and then on grass.

4. As you cross the broad saddle, keep to the left when the path forks, curving to the right beneath the rocks of Eel Crag. Ignore the path to the left, instead picking up a path beside the gill, heading south up the narrowing valley between Eel Crag and Grasmoor. At a **grassy saddle**, go left at a junction of paths, climbing to the **summit of Eel Crag (Crag Hill on the map)** on a path that's well cairned higher up.

5. Leave the summit **triangulation pillar**, heading southeast now, following a faint path that soon develops and curves down a rocky ridge above Scott Crag. Cross a small saddle, continuing

Leaving Grisedale Pike, heading for Hopegill Head and Eel Crag

ahead uphill towards the top of **Sail**. Cut left here, leaving the main path. The angle soon eases to reach the **summit cairn**.

6. Return to the main path a little further on, and turn left along it. Descend to cross over a saddle, and continue ahead at the junction of paths, before climbing up to the ridge of **Scar Crags**. Follow a fainter path to the **summit cairn**.

7. Continue eastwards, descending over the final saddle of the day, then climb steeply uphill over several bumps to **Causey Pike**.

8. Care is needed descending from Causey Pike in the direction of **Rowling End** below.

The initial descent down a steep rock rib is scrambly and exposed. Ignore the gully on the left, staying on the main rocks and dropping down to pick up a good path. Follow this down to a **cairn**, going left where the path forks, before descending to the left of Rowling End in the direction of **Stoneycroft Gill**.

Walk down this path towards **Stoneycroft Farm**, keeping the gill below to your left. When the path forks,

bear left, descending to the road beside a **bridge**.

9. Turn left over the bridge and follow the road past a parking area on the right and a quarry on the left.

Shortly before a plantation, turn left at a bridleway sign. Rise through gorse to the left of the plantation with a wall on your right. Climb over the end of the long northeast ridge of **Barrow** before descending across open ground to a gate. Walk down the next field to cross a stile between **farm buildings**. Curve right and left in front of the farm, then walk down the access track to the road.

(Alternatively you can cut this last section out and continue along the lane to Braithwaite.)

Turn left into **Braithwaite** and cross the bridge. Follow the road signposted to 'Whinlatter Pass', rising to turn left at a T-junction. Walk uphill along the busy road back to the quarry car park to complete the walk. ♦

High Snab Bank and Robinson from the Newlands road

Little Dale Round

Newlands Church – High Snab Bank – Robinson – Little Dale Edge – Hindscarth – Scope End – Low Snab

What to expect:
Narrow grassy ridges and broad summit plateau. A mix of grassy and stony paths

Distance: 10.5 kilometres/6½ miles

Ascent/descent: 790 metres/2,590 feet

Start: Free parking in a parking area on the minor road near Chapel Bridge, south of the hamlet of Little Town. This soon fills up, so get there early

Grid ref: NY 232 194

Ordnance Survey Map: OL 4 The English Lakes North-western area. *Keswick, Cockermouth & Wigton*

Wainwrights: Robinson, Hindscarth

Walk outline

After passing the beautiful Newlands Church, quiet lanes, access tracks and mountain paths take the walker onto the narrow ridge of High Snab Bank, where you can also enjoy a scramble up several rocky steps before the summit of Robinson is reached. The route stays high around Little Dale Edge to the summit of Hindscarth with a return along the wonderful Scope End ridge to complete an atmospheric and classic Lakeland horseshoe walk.

Little Dale Round

Robinson and Hindscarth enclose the hidden valley of Little Dale and are very similar in character, especially their northeast ridges. Both High Snab Bank and Scope End are classic Lakeland ridges — long and narrow with stunning views down either side. Views into the Buttermere valley can be enjoyed from Robinson, and to the Honister Pass and Newlands from Hindscarth.

You're likely to be accompanied all day by that ubiquitous 'little brown bird' of the uplands, the meadow pipit.

Newlands Church

Meadow pipit

The Walk

1. Leave the parking area and turn left over **Chapel Bridge**. Take the turning on the left signed to 'Newlands Church ¼ mile – No Through Road' and walk down the road to **Newlands Church**.

2. Ignore a left turn, and continue past the church with **Keskadale Beck** to your right. The farm road climbs gradually to a National Trust sign on the right for **'High Snab Farm'**. Keep ahead here. Higher up, go through a gate passing **Low High Snab** on the left. The track becomes rougher, passing through a gate after the buildings. Continue through another gate and carry on into **Little Dale**.

When the wall on the right ends, turn right, off the track, on a path that rises half-left steeply uphill, passing to the left of conifers. Continue climbing, to gain the ridge of **High Snab Bank**.

Walk left along the grassy crest of the ridge with grand views.

At the end of the ridge, the higher slopes of Robinson rise more steeply and four rocky steps have to be scrambled over. The path remains good and the way over the rocks is easy to follow. Stay on the main path above the scramble, ignoring any right turnings, to the **summit of Robinson**.

Continue over the summit area to the twin rock outcrops that mark the highest point.

3. Head south from Robinson, reaching a cairn near the **ridge fence**. Bear left on the path beside the fence. Descend to the grassy saddle of **Littledale Edge** at the head of Little Dale, where the path forks.

Take the lefthand fork, rising towards Hindscarth. The path curves to the right and peters out. Walk a few paces forward to another path and bear left to reach the **Hindscarth summit cairn**.

4. Leave the summit, heading north for a large **cairn-cum-shelter**. Pass this, dropping steeply down the hillside to join the narrow ridge of **Scope End**.

A delightful ridge path follows, sticking mostly to the crest. The final section of the ridge undulates before dropping steeply to arrive at a T-junction of paths near a fence and wall.

5. Bear right, following the path to the right of a **farmhouse**.

Beyond a **spoil heap**, curve left and descend to a track. Ignore the first footpath to the left, and take the permissive path signposted for 'Newlands Church', which heads left through the farmyard of **Low Snab**.

6. Follow the track beyond the farm to cross a **bridge**. When a lane joins from the left, continue ahead to reach **Newlands Church**. Turn right, back to the car park, to complete the walk. ◆

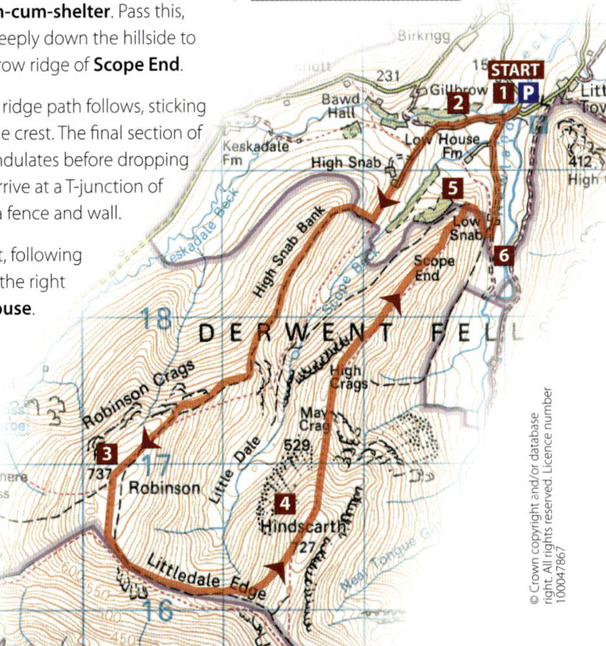

Looking down to The Rigg and Haweswater

High Street by Rough Crag

*The Rigg – Rough Crag – Long Stile End – High Street –
Rampsgill Head – Kidsty Pike – Kidsty Howes*

What to expect:
A mixture of grassy and rocky fell paths on a broad ridge.

Distance: 10 kilometres/6½ miles

Ascent/descent: 850 metres/2,800 feet

Start: Car park at the head of Haweswater.

Grid ref: NY 469 107

Ordnance Survey Map: OL 5 The English Lakes North-eastern area.
Penrith, Patterdale & Caldbeck

Wainwrights: High Street, Rampsgill Head, and Kidsty Pike

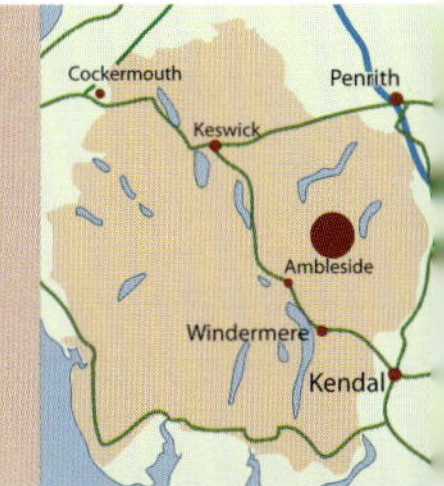

Walk outline

*A long, but not too demanding walk up a distinctive ridge with
fine views and a steep final climb to High Street. This is followed
by straightforward walking around the deeply-cut Riggindale
and over Kidsty Pike.*

High Street

Think of High Street and no vivid mountain image comes
to mind as it does with the mention of Blencathra, Skiddaw
or the Langdale Pikes. High Street is hidden amongst the
high moors of the northeastern fells: a high, Pennine-like
plateau, cut by long glacial valleys but with no memorable
skylines. Yet, up close, High Street provides fine drama, with
narrow ridges, high crags and deep mountain lakes.

Without doubt, the finest approach to High Street is along
the narrow edge of Rough Crag, the dramatic fall into
Riggindale on one side and the spectacular amphitheatre
holding Blea Water on the other.

The fells are home to that archetypal Lakeland breed of
sheep, the tough, brown-woolled Herdwick.

The Rigg

Herdwick sheep

The Walk

1. Go through the **gate** at the end of the little car park and follow the broad path ahead. In 100 metres or so, at a path junction, turn right at the corner of the wall and follow the path over **two footbridges**. Bear right after the second bridge and soon you will be walking above the lake towards the wooded headland known as '**The Rigg**'. As you approach the woods the path bears left up to the crest of the ridge. Go through a gap in the wall and bear left almost immediately to start the long ascent of the **Rough Crag ridge**.

There are grand views down the length of Haweswater as well as down into Riggindale and across to the shapely summit of Kidsty Pike.

The path is easy and ascends with the wall on the left until it passes through a gap in the wall. Steeper now, the path climbs up to gain the crest again by the wall. Once you are over this section the walking is much easier and you can cruise along and enjoy the widening views on both sides.

To the left you will see the two tarns of Small Water and Blea Water in their dark glacial valleys. Blea Water's claim to fame is its depth — at 63 metres/207 feet, it is the deepest tarn in the Lake District by a long way and of the larger valley lakes is only exceeded in depth by Wast Water and Windermere.

On the crest of Rough Crag looking to High Street

2. A small cairn marks the **summit of Rough Crag** after which the ridge drops to a small grassy saddle known as **Caspel Gate** where there is a **small pool**. Ahead the ridge steepens again for the final 200 metres climb up **Long Stile Edge** to the summit. The ridge is steep and rough but there is no difficulty and you are soon on the summit, its broad, grassy plateau coming as an anticlimax after the shapely ridge of the ascent.

3. The summit of **High Street** is marked by an Ordnance Survey **triangulation pillar**, but the views are better from here where you can look back down the ridge to Haweswater and into the shadowy depths of Blea Water over 300 metres below.

Head north on the good path along the ridge beside the wall and across the head of **Riggindale**, then bear northeast where the path forks to the broad bulky **summit of Rampsgill Head**. Continue to the fine little summit of **Kidsty Pike** with its superb views into Riggindale and across to Rough Crag and High Street.

4. From Kidsty Pike a good path descends almost due east for 1.5 kilometres/1 mile before heading down through the broken rocks of **Kidsty Howes**. Lower down, just above the lake, you pass close to **Randale Beck** on the left before bearing right to cross the **stone bridge** over **Riggindale Beck**. Follow the well-used footpath back beside the woods of **The Rigg** to complete the route. ♦

Looking down Mosedale to Yewbarrow from the shoulder of Pillar

Mosedale Horseshoe

Wasdale Head – Black Sail Pass – Pillar – Scoat Fell – Steeple – Red Pike – Yewbarrow

What to expect:
A long, spectacular ridge walk. High, rocky mountain paths. Short scramble

Distance: 17.25 kilometres/11 miles

Ascent/descent: 1,630 metres/5,350 feet

Start: There is a large parking area at Wasdale Green, about 400m before the famous 'Wasdale Head Inn'

Grid ref: NY 186 084

Ordnance Survey Map: OL 4 The English Lakes North-western area. *Keswick, Cockermouth & Wigton and* OL 6 The English Lakes South-western area. *Coniston, Ulverston & Barrow-in-Furness*

Wainwrights: Pillar, Scoat Fell, Steeple, Red Pike, Yewbarrow

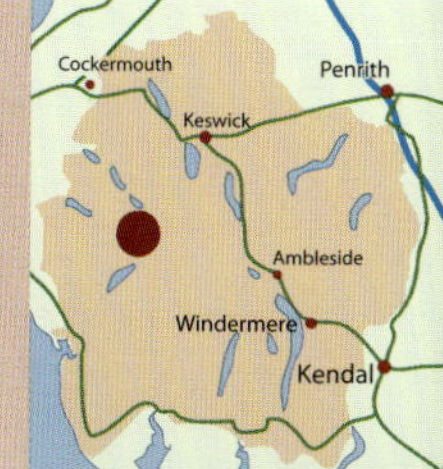

Walk outline

A gradual climb on a good path from Wasdale Head to Black Sail Pass is followed by a high-level ridge walk over Pillar, Scoat Fell and the striking rock peak of Steeple. The broad ridge continues to Red Pike and finally a scramble both onto and off the superb little mountain of Yewbarrow to complete the round.

Mosedale Horseshoe

Wasdale Head is one of the most famous centres for walking and climbing in the region. Its reputation is well earned: it's the wildest valley head in the Lake District, surrounded by the highest summits. But most eyes turn to either Scafell Pike (the highest peak in England) or Great Gable, leaving one of the finest horseshoe walks in the region unnoticed and almost untouched little more than a stone's throw away.

This is a superb route over high ground, gathering a fine collection of Lakeland summits along the way and enjoying unrivalled views of the Scafell group throughout.

Look out, too, for the elusive ring ouzel, a black bird with a white collar that nests among the rocks and boulder fields.

Black Sail YHA

Ring ouzel

The Walk

1. From **Wasdale Green** follow the lane to the 'Wasdale Head Inn'. Turn left through the car park, past the **shop and bar**, and bear right beside the beck. Pass the picturesque little **stone bridge** continuing ahead between the beck and a farm on the right. Soon the path splits — bear left rising to a gate where the Mosedale path swings left again.

Soon you are in the wilds of Mosedale and you can appreciate just how large and impressive it is for the first time. At the head of the dale the south face of Pillar rises in a series of steep broken crags over 700 metres, with the craggy eastern face of Red Pike to the left.

The path soon curves rightwards to begin the long climb to **Black Sail Pass**. Once you have crossed **Gatherstone Beck** the view back down the valley becomes increasingly impressive as the northern

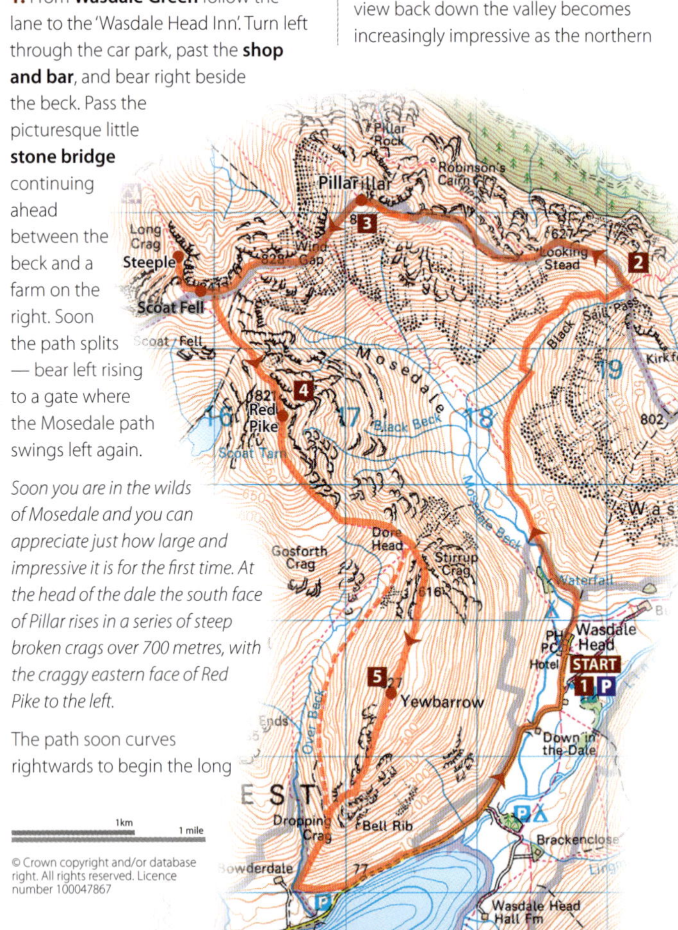

Walkers detour from the main ridge to the spectacular rock peak of Steeple

prow of Yewbarrow soars 500 metres above the beck.

2. As you reach the summit of the pass, the extensive view into Ennerdale is not realised, so head left along the ridge making the minor detour right to the **summit of Looking Stead** and all will be revealed — *the shadowy forested depths of Ennerdale, the Haystacks/ High Stile ridge, with Fleetwith Pike and the Robinson/Hinscarth ridge beyond. Southwards, is the striking prow of Yewbarrow.*

Continue steeply up the ridge from Looking Stead to the **summit of Pillar**, where you will enjoy spectacular views into both Ennerdale and Mosedale from the ridge.

Pillar has one of the best panoramas in the Lake District, a prospect dominated mainly by the jumbled, rocky mass of the Scafell group to the southeast, with the distinctive profile of Great Gable seen over the rounded back of Kirk Fell. Westwards, the view takes in the long glacial trough of Ennerdale culminating in Ennerdale Water with the Irish Sea in the distance.

3. From Pillar, head southwest over the extensive summit plateau and descend

Looking to Yewbarrow from Pillar, as the rising sun catches the ridge crest

into **Wind Gap**, the pass separating Pillar from Black Crag. The climb to **Black Crag** is broken and rocky but soon over and the remaining ridge to **Scoat Fell** is narrow and grassy with just a short rise over rocks to the summit, an unremarkable stony plateau.

The out-and-back extension to the superb summit of **Steeple** is recommended. The sight of Steeple as you approach along the ridge backed by Ennerdale and High Stile is one of the highlights of the walk.

Return to Scoat Fell and head southeast to pick up the ridge path to **Red Pike**.

Again the view is dominated by the Scafell group across the divide of Wasdale.

4. The descent from Red Pike to the pass of **Dore Head** is a mix of grass and scree, a good, visible path all the way.

(The Yewbarrow scramble can be by-passed here by turning right and following the path above Over Beck.)

The ascent of **Yewbarrow** is a straightforward walk up the broken, loose slope to begin the short scramble onto the ridge. The easiest line is on the left edge of the crags almost overlooking the drop into Mosedale.

There is less exposure to the right but the scrambling is less straightforward.

The summit ridge gives unrivalled views of the Scafell group, Great Gable and Wast Water.

5. The descent is initially straightforward and heads down the narrowing ridge with superb views to Wast Water over 500 metres below. Lower down look for the point where the path breaks right above **Dropping Crag. This is important as there is no walking route down the ridge crest from here.**

The descent is now steep and loose and you may doubt you are in the right place, but the path is obvious and there is a short section of **formalised pitching** lower down.

At the bottom of the scree a path heads left through the bracken to cross a **ladder stile** on the grassy ridge crest. Head right down the grass path beside the wall to a second stile. Turn left here and follow the path down beside **Over Beck** to the little car park.

The return to Wasdale Head is unavoidably along the road — just over 2 kilometres/1½ miles to complete the route. ♦

Perfect conditions on Striding Edge

Striding & Swirral Edges

Patterdale – Lanty's Tarn – Hole-in-the-Wall – Striding Edge – Helvellyn – Swirral Edge – Catstycam – Glenridding

What to expect:
Spectacular rocky ridge scramble in ascent and descent. Good, well used fell paths

Distance: 12 kilometres/7½ miles

Ascent/descent: 960 metres/3,150 feet

Start: The National Park car park in the centre of Glenridding.

Grid ref: NY 385 169

Ordnance Survey Map: OL 5 The English Lakes North-eastern area. *Penrith, Patterdale & Caldbeck*

Wainwright summits: Helvellyn, Catstycam

Walk outline

Easy walking to Lanty's Tarn to gain the Grisedale path followed by a long moderate ascent to the ridge crest. Straightforward low-grade scrambling on a narrow rock ridge with some exposure to reach Helvellyn's high summit plateau. A shorter scrambling descent via Swirral Edge, then easier walking to the shapely summit of Catstycam. The long easy-angled Glenridding path provides a return route.

Striding Edge & Swirral Edge

The most famous and popular mountains and hills in any area are usually the highest — Snowdon in North Wales, Ben Nevis in Scotland — but in the Lake District Helvellyn seems to have jumped the queue and knocked Scafell Pike off the number one spot. One reason for this is undoubtedly the inaccessibility of the latter. Helvellyn, on the other hand, rises directly from a main road which runs through the heart of the district. It is also one of the four highest summits in the Lake District and it has perhaps the most famous ridge walk in the country — Striding Edge. This narrow airy arête is justifiably famous and provides one of the best mountain experiences to be had on the Lakeland fells.

On Swirral Edge

Lichen

Walkers following the narrow crest of Striding Edge

The Walk

1. Leave the car park by the lower entrance and turn right along the road to cross the **bridge**. Turn right immediately (opposite the 'Glenridding **Hotel**') and walk along the lane between the river and the shops.

At the end of the access lane by **stone house**s, go left over the **footbridge** and follow the pitched footpath up through **woods**. Leaving the woods the path veers right across the open hillside.

2. At a gate in the **wall ahead,** don't go through; instead turn sharp left and follow the path up to **Lanty's Tarn**, in its small hollow and surrounded by pines.

Follow the path past the tarn, then bear right off the main path on a narrower footpath that heads across grass to enter and pass through a **small wood** by gates. Beyond the wood the path descends to join the main path coming up from **Grisedale**.

Grisedale is a beautiful valley and there are superb views from here up to the head of the dale to the shapely summits of Nethermost Pike, Dollywaggon Pike and St Sunday Crag.

Turn right and follow the broad path climbing steadily up towards the famous '**Hole-in-the-Wall**' — a gap in the wall that can be seen running up the hillside to the skyline ahead. The path is never steep, but it is much further than it looks to the skyline (over 2 kilometres/1½ miles).

As you gain height there are increasing views left into Grisedale and up to the head of the valley.

The ridge crest is a good place for a break. Here the impressive east face of Helvellyn, with the enclosing arms of Striding Edge and Swirral Edge, can be seen for the first time rising above Red Tarn which occupies the bottom of the combe (out of sight until you are further along the ridge).

3. Cross the stile here ('Hole in the Wall') and continue on the path ahead. **Striding Edge** starts with the small **summit of Low Spying How**, a good place to take stock of the ridge ahead.

The first section is composed of clean blocky rock with very little grass, the second half is narrower with a sharper

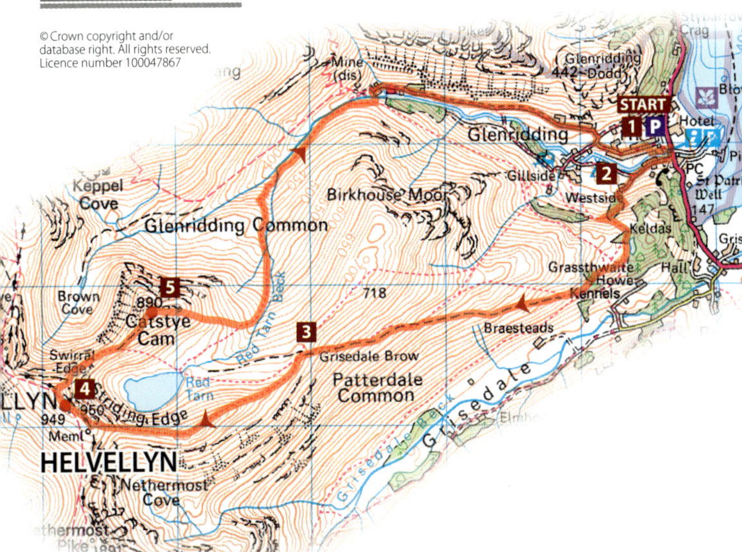

Scramblers on the crest of Striding Edge with views to St Sunday Crag and Fairfield

crest but more broken rocks. **NB –** Nowhere is the scrambling 'difficult' but it is fairly exposed, so you will need good balance and a head for heights. **The less adventurous can avoid the crest by a traversing path a little way down on the right.**

The final obstacle on the ridge provides the crux — a **squat rock tower** requiring a short scramble descent to a narrow gap at the point where the ridge merges into the broken upper slopes of the mountain. Easier scrambling, then steep scree lead onto the summit plateau where you will enjoy the fine classic view back along the ridge.

Head right along the plateau rim past the cross-shaped **stone wind shelter** to **Helvellyn summit**.

Helvellyn is one of the few Lakeland summits where almost every other fell is visible. The most striking panorama is westwards, where you should be able to see the Coniston Fells, Bowfell, Crinkle Crags, Esk Pike and Scafell Pike. Great Gable is probably the most prominent and striking of all. The Derwent Fells and Skiddaw complete the view to the northwest.

4. Beyond the summit a small **cairn** marks the exit point from the plateau

onto **Swirral Edge**. This is both easier and shorter than Striding Edge, but still requires care. The broken rocks soon merge into grass as the angle eases on the broad saddle between Helvellyn and Catstycam.

A good path bears right from here to the outflow of **Red Tarn** where it joins the Glenridding path, but Catstycam is too good a summit to leave out and is easily gained by the gentle ridge ahead.

The view back to Helvellyn rising above Red Tarn from here is superb, particularly under winter conditions, or when late snow lingers on this sheltered northeast face.

5. From the **summit of Catstycam**, descend the rounded east ridge on the path that sweeps down to join the Glenridding path beside **Red Tarn Beck**.

Follow this path down beside the beck into the lower valley. The path then stays close to the broader **Glenridding Beck**. Cross the beck by the large **wooden footbridge** on the left and follow the path right, soon passing **Glenridding Youth Hostel** to join the unsurfaced lane which can be followed easily back to **Glenridding** to complete the route (about 2 kilometres/1½ miles). ♦

Scramblers on Sharp Edge

SCRAMBLE

Blencathra's ridges

*Scales – Mousthwaite Comb - Scales Tarn – Sharp Edge
Blencathra – Hall's Fell Ridge – Gate Gill – Doddick Gill*

What to expect:
*Spectacular rocky ridge
scramble in ascent and
descent with exposure.
Good fell paths*

Distance: 9 kilometres/5½ miles
Ascent/descent: 722 metres/2,370 feet
Start: Limited parking is available in a layby on the A66 at Scales
(grid ref: NY 344 269). Alternatively there is a small parking area
along the minor lane about 700 metres beyond the 'White Horse
Inn' at Scales. Park immediately after the little bridge
Grid ref: NY 349 272
Ordnance Survey Map: OL 5 The English Lakes North-eastern area.
Penrith, Patterdale & Caldbeck
Wainwrights: Blencathra (Hallsfell Top)

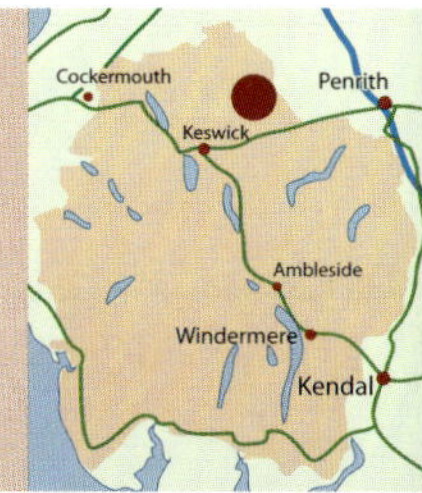

Walk outline

*Initially steep walking on good footpaths leads over the
broad grassy ridge of Scales Fell and beside the upper River
Glenderamackin to reach the sheltered hollow containing
Scales Tarn directly below Sharp Edge. Exposed scrambling
on Sharp Edge takes you directly onto the summit plateau.
Descent is by the easier but still rocky edge of Hall's Fell
Ridge — a direct and spectacular 600 metre line down the
mountain's southern face. Easy walking to finish.*

Blencathra's ridges

Blencathra is the great mountain bulk that greets the
motorist entering the Lake District from the northeast
along the A66. And what a greeting — no gentle
introductions, this mountain hits you like a fist and reveals
all in a magnificent medley of ridges and buttresses.

This route uses easy access from the A66 for a classic round
via Sharp Edge and Hall's Fell Ridge. Sharp Edge is one of
the best low-end scrambles in the Lake District and takes a
direct line up a narrow rock ridge. If you enjoy Sharp Edge,
Hall's Fell Ridge provides the logical descent being easier
and less exposed, but still providing interesting scrambling.

Scales Tarn

Peregrine and prey

The Walk

1. From the main road follow the lane past the '**White Horse Inn**' and just before it bends left down to cross a stream, take the signed path on the left.

The path is well used and obvious and heads up the left-hand side of the little valley of **Mousthwaite Comb**, before swinging diagonally-right across the steep valley head to the broad saddle on the skyline.

The saddle is a good place to take a breather and survey the route ahead. Sharp Edge can be seen rising impressively above the upper valley of the River Glenderamackin with the rounded, grassy shoulder of Scales Fell to the left.

2. The path swings left now along the broad grassy saddle towards **Scales Fell** and in about 400 metres forks. The path ahead continues up the broad, gentle slopes of Scales Fell to reach the summit. **Note:** *If you have any doubts about Sharp Edge, this is a straightforward route to the summit.*

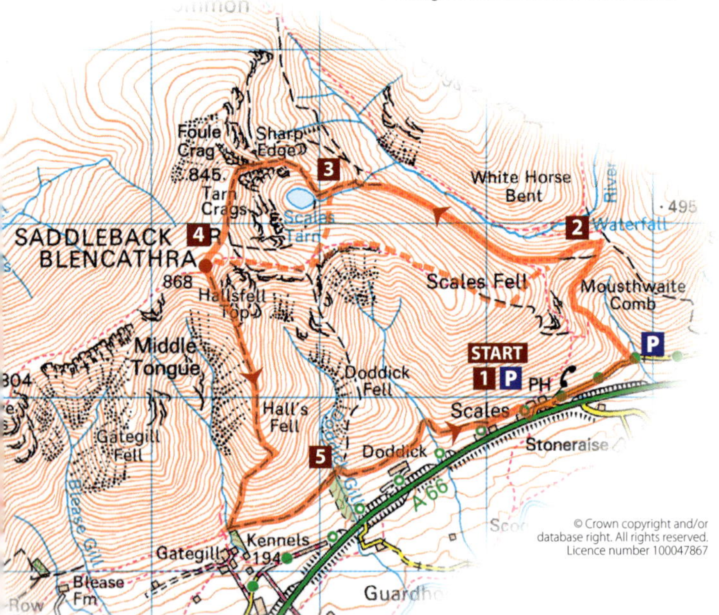

Looking down the final section of Sharp Edge ridge scramble

For **Sharp Edge**, branch right at the fork and follow the path on a contouring line up the valley towards the saddle on the skyline separating **Blencathra** from **Bannerdale Crags**, with the beck down to the right.

About halfway up the valley the path crosses **Scales Beck**, which cascades out of the unseen hollow above. Cross the stream, then bear left up the pitched path beside the beck to **Scales Tarn**.

3. Over 150 metres above the tarn, **Sharp Edge** strikes an impressive skyline fringed by broken rock slabs and steep screes. Head right up the steep approach path to the start of the ridge. (If you have a change of heart, the path up steps to the left at the tarn outflow will take you up the easier Scales Fell route.)

Scrambling is easy at first and begins up a 'V' shaped groove to reach the narrow crest. The ridge crest is quite narrow and there is exposure on both sides, but the scrambling is straightforward and much of it can be walked with just the occasional steadying hand if you feel confident enough.

Sharp Edge is one of Lakeland's most challenging ridge scrambles

The central section resembles a rock pavement but the polished rock can be slippery in the wet. The crux comes just before the ridge joins the main bulk of the mountain where some **small pinnacles** must be passed. The easiest line bypasses them on the right by means of a sloping ledge which some may find intimidating on account of the drop into a gully on the right. This can be slippery in the wet and requires care. The alternative is by delicate moves over a considerable drop on the left-hand side of the crest.

This leads to a gap in the ridge before the final slabby rocks that lead up onto the summit. Either climb these direct on good rock with small holds, or a slightly easier line can be taken up a shallow gully a few metres to the right.

The scrambling ends almost on the summit plateau where a good path heads left along the top of **Tarn Crags** to the **summit of Blencathra**.

The view from here is superb — especially down the 600 metre south face of the mountain. Just about every Lakeland fell of note is visible, from the Coniston Fells past Bowfell, Scafell Pike, Great Gable, the Buttermere and Derwent Fells, to the neighbouring giant of Skiddaw.

. The 600-metre-long **Hall's Fell Ridge** makes the perfect descent, being easier nd more straightforward than Sharp dge with little, if any, of the latter's xposure. It is also easy to locate, even n poor visibility, as it falls directly from ne summit. The upper half of the ridge ontains almost all of the scrambling vhich can be varied at will or even voided altogether by paths mainly to ne left of the crest.

The Scales Fell path [due east] is a traightforward alternative descent.)

he lower section of the ridge is steep ather than rocky, the path trending ght to reach the stream of **Gate Gill**

with walled fields ahead and a small wood. Don't cross the stream here, but instead turn sharp left and follow the good footpath parallel to the wall on the right.

5. After you cross the next stream (**Doddick Gill)**, you will need to make an unexpected rise around the **walled fields** ahead to continue.

The final obstacle is a short scramble down a rock step to cross **Scaley Beck**. About 400 metres further on, take the path right, between cottages, to reach the main road where a left turn will take you back to the **White Horse Inn** to complete the route. ◆

Useful Information

Cumbria Tourism

Cumbria Tourism's official website covers everything from accommodation and events to attractions and adventure. **www.golakes.co.uk**

Lake District National Park

The Lake District National Park website also has information on things to see and do, plus maps, webcams and news. **www.lakedistrict.gov.uk**

Tourist Information Centres

The main TICs provide free information on everything from accommodation and travel to what's on and walking advice.

Ambleside	01539 432 582	tic@thehubofambleside.com
Bowness	01539 442 895	bownesstic@lake-district.gov.uk
Coniston	01539 441 533	mail@conistontic.org
Keswick	01768 772 645	keswicktic@lake-district.gov.uk
Penrith	01768 867 466	pen.tic@eden.gov.uk
Ullswater	01768 482 414	ullswatertic@lake-district.gov.uk
Windermere	01539 446 499	windermeretic@southlakeland.gov.uk

Emergencies

The Lake District is covered by twelve volunteer mountain rescue teams. In a real emergency:

1. Make a note of your location (with OS grid reference, if possible); the name, age and sex of the casualty; their injuries; how many people are in the group; and your mobile phone number.

2. Call 999 or 112 and ask for the Cumbria police, and then for Mountain Rescue

3. Give them your prepared details.

4. Do NOT change position until contacted by the mountain rescue team.

Weather

Five day forecast for the Lake District: 0844 846 2444
www.lakedistrict.gov.uk/weatherline